I WONDER...

About The Sky

by
Enid Field

photographs
by Florence Harrison

AN ELK GROVE BOOK

 CHILDRENS PRESS, CHICAGO

Photographic Special Credits:

Ed Field — hummingbird
Elmer Steiner — lightning

Library of Congress Cataloging in Publication Data

Field, Enid.
  I wonder . . . about the sky.

  SUMMARY: Black and white photographs accompany
verses about the sky.

  "An Elk Grove book."

  [1. American poetry] I. Harrison, Florence, 1910-
illus. II. Title.
PZ8.3.F4553Iay   811' .5'4   72-10205
ISBN 0-516-07622-1

1 2 3 4 5 6 7 8 9 10 11 12 13 14 15 16 17 18 19 20 21 22 23 24 25 R 75 74 73

I WONDER...

About The Sky

I WONDER...

why I like to lie
on my back and watch the sky,
and see cloud-monsters chase away
fluffy animals at play?

I WONDER...

how the sun can play
the morning trick it does each day,
making day come out of night,
changing dark to yellow light?

I WONDER...

when I jump up high
if I can reach and touch the sky,
and feel if it is soft and cool
like the water in a pool?

I WONDER...

if somebody knows
where the big sky really goes;
where it starts and where it ends,
and if the earth and sky are friends?

I WONDER...

when I get to fly
in a plane across the sky,
if I will look down here and see
my friends all looking up at me?

I WONDER...

when the windmill goes,
turning with each wind that blows,
is it a pinwheel in the sky
for every wind that passes by?

I WONDER...

if the sky out there
is making something else to wear
as fancy as the lace I see
hanging on this leafy tree?

I WONDER...

how the birds can fly
and not bump others in the sky,
with no signs to let them know
when to STOP and when to GO?

I WONDER...

if snowflakes I see
that all look so alike to me,
can be as different as they say,
with each one made in its own way?

I WONDER...

if the moon can be
a place my cat would like to see;
and will there be moon mice to chase
away up there in outer space?

I WONDER...

where the kite will go
when a big wind starts to blow
if it isn't held to land
by a string in someone's hand?

I WONDER...

when the lightning streaks
all around the mountain peaks,
if it's a flashlight for the sky
to use until the storm goes by?

I WONDER...

if the raindrops race
to find a happy landing place,
when they hurry down to play
from a stormy sky of gray?

I WONDER...

when I reach the top
of this big tree and have to stop,
if I can give the sky a pat,
or is it still too high for that?

I WONDER...

if the hummer found
that downy feather on the ground;
or did she see it in the sky
and catch it as it floated by?

I WONDER...

where reflections go
when the sun is getting low?
Do they sink or float away,
or wait here for another day?

I WONDER...

why I always try
to find the first star in the sky,
to "wish I may, and wish I might
have the wish I wish tonight"?

I WONDER...

why I like to lie
in my bed and watch the sky
and feel its darkness gently creep
around me as I go to sleep?